Scribbles... In Waiting

Tejas Ingale

India | USA | UK

Presentation by *BookLeaf Publishing*

Web: www.bookleafpub.com

E-mail: info@bookleafpub.com

ISBN: 9789363318991

First edition 2024

DEDICATION

This book is dedicated to:

My father, Nitin - for inculcating in me the habit of being observant.

My mother, Neha - for teaching me how to aspire to reach my dreams.

My wife, Anagha - for always being there by my side and for motivating me throughout.

My dog, Miso - for being the world's best stress-buster and antidepressant.

PREFACE

Have you ever had to wait to get anything done?
Be it as simple as eating at a restaurant? Or
maybe you have a meeting but the client is
busy? Or perhaps, you are on a long-distance
flight? Have you had a medical appointment but
the doctor was with another patient? The wait
can feel long, time slow. Is your mind full of
thoughts? Are you bored? What do you do then?
Bury your head in your phone? Read a
magazine? Or maybe, just maybe, open your
eyes and ears and observe around you?

Scribbles... During Visa Application

To go abroad, you need a visa,
Be it to Ukraine or the Pyramids of Giza.
If you want to go from Berlin to Paris,
Either by train or while driving a Yaris.
Each country's visa application procedure,
Varies in process and expenditure.
Visa-on-arrival available in some places,
Just pop up at the border in dedicated spaces.
Pay the fees, and you're done, free to enter,
The easiest one of the lot, absolute splendor.
Other countries may have e-visa facilities,
Apply from your own home, easy capability.
Upload all documents, pay the fees,
Get the visa in your email with absolute ease.
For other countries, the process is a fair bit longer,
Your application docket must also be stronger.

Choose the type of visa, decide your stance,
Prepare all the documents well in advance.
Based on your purpose of visit and events,
You may need to prepare over twenty
documents.
Once they are ready, you make an appointment,
Physically, you visit the application center then.
Luggage, electronics, and other things not
allowed,
Stand in a queue with the rest of the crowd.
Based on your scheduled time, they let you in,
Pass through security and some frisking.
You can sit in a lounge should you wish,
Pay additional fees in order to avail this.
Go inside, and you take out a token,
Then wait around till you're called for
submission.
In a normal area, there are just chairs to sit,
Maybe a water cooler, and that's it.
Additional facilities available inside the lounge,
To help you relax till your number comes
around.
You can pour yourself a cup of coffee,
And have along with it a biscuit or cookie.
A packet of crisps is something you can eat,
Or maybe have a chocolate as you sit in your
seat.
Someone comes and helps you arrange your
documents,

To ensure everything is in order when,
You go to the counter when it's your number,
And submit all documents in the correct order.
Should anything be missing, they will tell you then,
You can send the missing ones by email.
Even once you're done with the submission,
Your job here is still not done.
To another room, you must go,
Where they will click your photo.
They will also take your fingerprints,
Biometrics is what they call this thing.
This is the case when you don't have to,
Visit Embassy or Consulate for an interview.
The interview process is quite different,
Where you don't submit any document.
You take them all for your interview,
And answer any questions that they ask you.
Sometimes it is a very long wait,
Other times it is immediate.
Till you find out if you're successful,
In getting a visa, it is stressful.
Some people wait their entire lives,
For one single chance that they might,
Get to travel abroad, 'coz in the end,
Travelling is a unique experience, dear friend.

Scribbles... At an Airport

I'm sitting at the airport, waiting for my flight,
I'm really tired, it's quite late at night.
I left home early to beat the traffic,
If I'd hit it, I might've had it.
But I didn't, so here I am now,
Got to wait around, I don't know how.
So many people travelling, wanting to go places,
With fear, excitement and joy on their faces.
Somewhere there's a seafarer, joining his first
ship,

Someone's flying alone, embarking on a solo
trip.
Mom, dad, and two kids – a family of four,
And there's a big group, of ten, maybe more.
Someone's waited their whole life to even see a
flight,
Another's travelled so much, this is a common
sight.
There seems to be a commotion at one of the
counters,
Someone's packed something that they perhaps
shouldn't've.
The good, the bad and the ugly, it's all there to
see,
Everyone's flying, they've all got somewhere to
be.
You may be a seasoned hand, or you may be
travelling new,
The rules are the same, for the many and for the
few.
It's funny really, should you stop to notice,
And not everyone seems to know this,
Inside an airport, there's a different concept of
time,
You can have dinner in the morning, can have a
drink at nine.
People wearing jeans and tees, or a suit, shirt
and tie,
It's all just a blur, like a blob floating by.

Some people happy, some in obvious pain,
Some wondering if and when they'll ever meet
again.
Submit your luggage, you won't need it,
Once you reach your destination, you will see it.
Take your essentials in a carry-on,
Those you may need when the flight is on.
Pillow, cash, documents and keys,
A book, a pen – paper, and type Cs.
You hope that your luggage does reach,
Your destination in one piece.
It just might get lost midway,
And may reach you in a couple of days.
Head to security after check-in,
Forbidden items go straight into the bin.
The rest can go through an X-Ray,
Remove everything in a separate tray.
Walk through a metal detector thing,
Lend yourself out to some frisking.
Suspicious items security will tag,
Explain them and repack your bag.
Then make your way to immigration,
To officially exit that particular nation.
Shop if you wish at Duty Free,
Or perhaps you can get a bite to eat.
Or maybe make your way to the gate,
To board the flight, you must wait.
Don't be fooled by the glam and the glitz,
Or even by the expensive food and the fizz.

It's a surreal place, and I'll tell you why,
An airport's the place where you'll find the most
sincere goodbye.

Scribbles... In a Flight

Boarding was delayed but settled in place,
Seating three across in a congested space.
Some prefer the window, I prefer the aisle,
It's certainly more comfy than the middle file.
Weather is good, the takeoff was smooth,
Pretty soon we reached cruising altitude.
They brought the food quickly, they brought the drink,
And through it all, I started to think.
It's a long flight, what am I supposed to do?
I really should've brought a book or two.
Fifteen hours is too bloody long,
You can only see so many movies, listen to a few songs.
As I cast my gaze and look through bored eyes,
One prominent thing, I come to realize.

More than eight billion people, there are in this world,
Yet, three hundred of those sat in the same metal bird.
Every one of them had made the exact same plan,
To take off together, and together to land.
Coincidence, God's will, or whatever the case may be,
For this brief period of time, they're all family.
All going to the same place, eating the same food,
Some in a happy while some in a crap mood.
The man next to me, sitting shoeless,
To the baby two rows back, absolutely clueless.
Bang on cue, the baby starts to cry,
It's baffled parents start wondering why.
People trying to sleep, getting disturbed,
As soon as the baby's wails are heard.
A queue outside the toilet, everyone wants to go,
Smoking on a flight is a big no-no.
Some holding their breath, someone gives a sigh,
These are the issues with catching a red-eye.
Someone's catching a glimpse of their favourite show,
Someone's playing games with a neighbour in the next row.
Everyone has plans after getting off the flight,

Someone won't have connections, someone
might.
In the still silence, people manage to sleep,
Punctuated by the sound of an overhead beep.
A little bit of turbulence never brought down a
plane,
The attendants stay calm, no one's going insane.
WiFi on board helps you keep track of the score,
The guy next to me has started to snore.
I think I'll take a nap, I think it's the best,
Give my tired eyes some much-needed rest.
This flight just goes on, it just seems to last,
When I wake up, more time would've passed.
Eventually though, it'll be time to land,
And I hope everything goes according to plan.
I really do hope that the landing is smooth,
Sometimes it's scary to tell you the truth.
Well, bye for now, it is nap time,
I'm done with six hours, I still have nine.

Scribbles... In a Transit Lounge

I'm done with one flight, I've got one more,
Long-distance travel can be such a bore.
Go through transit, pass security,
And once again, go through all the scrutiny.
As if mid-flight, something I bought,
Dangerous, illegal, worthy of being caught.
Anyway, done with it, and here I am,
Don't worry though, 'coz I have a plan.
Every airport has something called a lounge,
To help you relax, unwind and calm down.
For right now I have a few hours to kill,
So to the lounge, make my way I will.
I'm so hungry, all the food I'll devour,
And maybe even have a nice, hot shower.

And not to mention, unlimited drinks,
And perhaps a place to catch a wink.
I grab a table by the window,
And look outside and down below.
Flights taking off and coming to land,
Ground staff providing a helping hand.
Different flights, with a different livery,
Some exciting, while some pretty dreary.
Fuelling being done in one scene,
Another flight loading the on-board meal.
Ground staff waving their hands in the air,
Some with a light, others bare.
Looking inside, the music is good,
And a long counter with delicious food.
Multi-cuisine is the menu of the day,
Japanese, Continental and Chhole Bhature.
Not to mention the salad, bread and soup,
And an entire table, just full of fruit.
Cornflakes, milk and coffee and tea,
And a big basket of cookies.
A chiller dispensing cubes of ice,
Some food mild, while some with spice.
A live bar open twenty-four-seven,
To have vodka with a dash of lemon.
If you fancy, you can even have a beer,
All types of alcohol are served here.
Don't forget to have some delicious dessert,
You eat so much, your insides hurt.
But don't worry, there are facilities for you,

Clean, hygienic, and easy to use.
Should you feel sleepy after all this food,
Recliner seats help you set the mood.
Perhaps, during daytime, you can take a nap,
Or maybe, at night, fancy a night-cap.
A TV showing all flight information,
A few more showing news from every nation.
No announcements are made, so, traveller,
beware,
Of your own flight, you must be aware.
So come on, enter, and take some rest,
Before your next flight, you can feel refreshed.
And the best thing is, for a reasonable fee,
Everything in the lounge is absolutely free.

Scribbles… Outside a Public Toilet

My predicament makes me wonder why,
I ever decided to catch a red-eye.
Knowing perfectly well that it would land,
At a time, difficult, in the day of man.
Waking up in the morning, what's the first thing
you do?
Don't be shy now, everyone else does it too.
Well, it seems everyone else got the sign,
That to do it now would be the best time.
As I make my way to use the loo,
I see that there is quite a queue.
At that moment, I had to take a call,

Do I wait in line to get a stall?
Or do I go and find another loo,
And hope it doesn't have as big a line too?
But what if that decision turns out to be wrong?
And the other place has a queue just as long?
Returning here would not be an option,
I would really have to proceed with caution.
So I decided to stay in place,
And hope that the queue moves at a pace.
This is where I'm standing, hoping it works out,
It's gonna be difficult, without a doubt.
Each passing minute feels like an hour,
The situation looks bleak, Aaaaaaargh!
I cast my mind to a simpler time,
When I was but a small child.
A situation like this wouldn't have mattered
then,
I could've just done it there and then.
Nobody else would've batted an eye,
If a small child would've pooped and cried.
The diaper that he's wearing takes care of it,
Even soiling one's pants is expected of it.
Things are way different when you're an adult,
Got to hold it, control it, to avoid an insult.
Soil as a child, people are understanding,
Soil beyond your tweens, it's embarrassing.
There's no recovering from something like that,
For days, weeks, years, and even beyond that.
This thing in itself can be traumatizing,

And no, I'm not simply dramatizing.
Now, some of you may be wondering,
Who takes a pen and paper during,
Standing in a queue for doing their business?
Well, guess what? That's not what this is.
This is being written on my mobile phone,
In order to get myself in the zone.
And distract myself from the situation,
The worry, the stress, and the tension.
But I don't really think that it is working,
And it probably won't, what am I thinking?
Trying to distract myself from something,
By writing about that very same thing.
A medley of sounds from every stall,
Some insensitive bloke's answering a call.
And not to mention the occasional smell,
Enough to make your life a living hell.
It's best really to just not think,
And have your mood positively sink.
You have to feel bad for the attendant,
Who has to clean up after each one.
By God's grace, the line has moved,
And hopefully, I'll go in, in a minute or two.
I knock on a door, someone says, "Just a
minute."
It's really funny now, 'innit?
Time as a thing is pretty relative,
Sometimes positive, sometimes negative.
During difficulty, it just doesn't end,

Having fun, an hour is a second.
In the end, one thing you have to understand,
You can be anywhere, in any foreign land.
How long a minute is really depends on,
The side of the door that you are on.

Scribbles... At Immigration

Landed safely, I've reached my destination,
In a far away place, a different nation.
Every single passenger gets down and
de-boards,
And makes their way to the same place, follows
the horde.
We're all heading to Passport Control, a.k.a.
Immigration,
Where everyone gets a stamp to officially enter a
nation.
We'll be joined by people from other flights,
Boy, does it seem like it's gonna be a long night.
Although the queue is pretty reasonable,
It doesn't look like anyone will be able,
To be done so soon, as is always common,
Only two counters are open, out of a dozen.
The immigration queue is a great leveller,
A family, solo, or business traveller,
From any country, city, village or town,

Standing in the same queue metres down.
Sometimes all passports are clubbed into one,
Sometimes they're split, other countries and
home.
People have in their hands, boarding pass and
passport,
Every single one is looking bored.
Different passports of a different colour,
The country's name displayed on the cover.
Japan, Russia, Qatar, Romania,
Chile, the US, Ghana, Albania.
Everyone decided to visit the same place,
All of them occupying the exact same space.
Everyone's bored now, it's taking too long,
There's nothing to do but to hold on.
People in wheelchairs getting priority,
Delaying the queue further, that ain't pretty.
A dad trying to play a game with his kid,
The kid's really tired, he wants to sit.
People are struggling to keep their calm,
Fear of repercussions holding them down.
Hurry up, man, we've got places to go,
How the hell can this be so slow?
After immigration, luggage we have to take,
Then, towards the exit, our way we have to
make.
Then take transport to further make our way,
And this just might spill over into the next day.

Scribbles... At a Railway Station

Travelling by train, I'm at the station,
The train's gonna take me across the nation.
I've gotten here early, I've got to wait,
The train hasn't arrived at the platform yet.
Unlike a flight that calls out your name,
A train leaves without you, just the same.
Whether you're on it or not, it just doesn't
matter,
It'll leave without you if you're busy in chatter.
So, arrive early, wait around if you need,
To the announcements made, pay good heed.
Many people waiting, doing the same,
Some travelling for the first time by train.

Young and old, people of all ages,
Describing everything would take many pages.
Luggage of different shapes and size,
Some have been here since sunrise.
Some people bored, sitting on a bench,
A mechanic moving around, in his hand a
wrench.
Friends passing time, chatting about stuff,
Boys running around, playing rough.
Railway canteen serving delicious food,
You have to try it once, it's really good.
Some people sleep in the intense heat,
On the hard-paved ground, on just a sheet.
Flies and mosquitoes flying merry,
Irritating everyone, including the weary.
Food stalls selling items to eat,
Mostly vegetarian, little to no meat.
Indian snacks – tested and tried,
Dhokla, bhujia and samosa fried.
Chocolates, biscuits, coffee and tea,
Some even selling some idli.
Juice, soft drinks, bottles of water,
People flock there as it gets hotter.
Bookstalls selling various books,
Fiction, non-fiction or comic books.
Travel essentials may also be sold,
A pillow and blanket for when you're cold.
Bars or strips of soap also,
So that you can wash your hands thorough.

Luggage being carried by a porter,
On his head, hands, and even his shoulder.
Cargo handlers hauling different cargo,
That is going to distance far go.
Cleaning personnel doing their duty,
To make the station a thing of beauty.
This includes the urinals and the toilet,
Most people just done go and soil it.
Station masters and their support staff,
Can't go and do their duties in half.
Everyone's safety depends on them,
Their job seriously they have to take then.
My train's announcement has just been made,
It's finally arriving a few hours late.
I've got to leave now, I hope you wish me,
For this train ride, a happy journey.

Scribbles... In a Train

The train is moving, it is pretty late,
And I'm struggling to sleep, which I hate.
Travelling by train could be fun,
Especially to schedule if it would run.
In your berth, you settle in,
Luggage under the seat you're putting.
Based on your compartment and the train,
Your experience of the journey just might
change.
I'm in 3rd AC, just so you know,
So this train of thought you could follow.

Your co-passengers are something to look out
for,
You hope they're not someone uncalled for.
Someone may have eaten before boarding the
train,
Others may bring more food to eat again.
You may be served on-board food,
If the train's services are that good.
Third AC has three berths, and at side two,
Second AC has an arrangement two-by-two.
As the train moves, you settle in,
There are sockets provided for charging.
Your phone, tablet, or laptop as well,
One for each berth, that's swell.
You may have carried the newspaper for today,
To catch up on what happened yesterday.
Or maybe read a book for the rest of the day,
Or play some games to pass the time away.
The train keeps stopping at various stations,
As it takes you through this great nation.
Some people getting on with their luggage and
stuff,
Others ending their journey and getting off.
Also getting on maybe some salesmen,
Selling their wares, hoping you'd get them.
Cell phone covers, cables, clips for your hair,
Packets of chips for people to share.
Samosa, vada and such fried food,
No alcohol allowed to set the mood.

Tea and coffee or maybe hot milk,
Or bottled water or some soft drink.
Lots of options for you to choose,
Washrooms available for you to use.
Indian and Western, both available,
Use whichever ones that you are able.
Flush, jet spray, or even a mug,
Keep them clean, don't be smug.
Be considerate to the next guy,
To not make a mess, you have to try.
A separate basin to wash your hands,
To use this though, you have to stand.
You're provided with a bedsheet, pillow and
blanket,
So you can have as much sleep as you can get.
The middle berth is a backrest,
Lift it up to form a bed.
Be aware, though, that if you raise it,
On the bottom berth, no one can sit.
The lower berth person, forced to lie down,
Or he would have to stand around.
The best berth to be is the uppermost one,
Just climb up and you are done.
The two on the side are equally good,
To sleep on the lower one, you should,
Drop the seat back to form a bed,
When you get up, just mind your head.
The side upper doesn't have a working fan,
Bear the heat and sweat, if you can.

Windows for you to look out from,
At the passing scenery, up and down.
Sometimes there may even be a curtain,
So that the outside light doesn't get in.
Overall the train journey is comfortable,
In spite of that, I still am unable,
To sleep; perhaps it's my body's caution,
To not subject it to severe exhaustion.

Scribbles... In a Metro

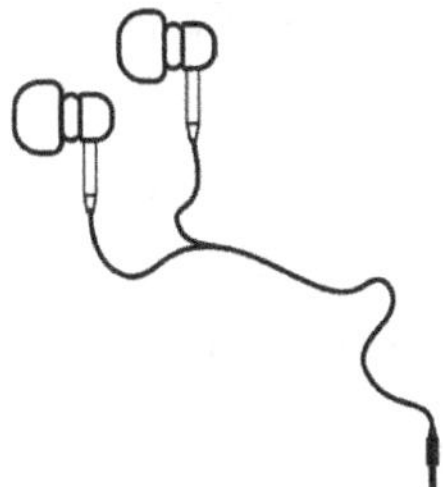

I'm travelling by metro, and this seems good,
It's been a long time coming, so of course it
would.
Public transport in this place was non-existent,
And people's destinations were a fair bit distant.
It had cultivated a typical mentality,
Of point-to-point service in all totality.
The situation on the roads is always a mess,
Traffic and pollution adding to the stress.
Hopefully, this thing will help alleviate,
The absolute mess that traffic creates.
The commute is comfortable, calm and relaxing,
The end of the day is much less taxing.
You can attend all calls and send an email,
And even conduct a big deal, down to the last
detail.
Friends can meet up to chat and greet,
Old folks can commute while resting their feet.

You can access social media, Instagram or
Facebook,
Or peer out the window to get a brand-new look.
Your own city now looks so different, so new,
A whole new vantage point sets your thoughts
anew.
And all of this while being safe, sound and
secure,
Putting no one in danger, that's for sure.
Texting while driving is dangerous as hell,
Texting in the metro, it's encouraged just as
well.
Talking on the phone while tilting your head,
Driving a bike like this, you might as well be
dead.
Talk as much as you want, even on speaker,
what the heck,
And you won't even have to strain your neck.
Public transport's good, it makes your life better,
It's cheap, it's affordable, it keeps us safe
together.
So make good use of it, but also take care,
Don't misuse or damage it, 'coz it just ain't fair.
If I were driving now, I wouldn't've had the
time,
Let alone the focus to come up with a rhyme.
Now that I'm here, my mind is free,
To wander, wonder, and think of any possibility.
Anti-social elements, please take note,

Please don't damage this now, try to be the
GOAT.
I'm quite happy, I don't know about you,
'Coz this thing here was damn overdue.

Scribbles... In a Bus

I'm travelling by bus, it's a new venture,
Every minute seems like a new adventure.
I've travelled before, don't get me wrong,
I've never travelled a distance this long.
Conventionally travelled by a normal seater,
This time it's an overnight sleeper.
Traditional seats, two-by-two,
Replaced by berths, one-by-two.
Up-and-down arrangement, like a bunk,
And luggage kept in an underneath trunk.
A seater trip lasts but a few an hour,
Sleepers travel to distances afar.
You board in the city from a suitable stop,
All buses then meet at a central spot.
Boarding late evening or early night,
At the central spot, most passengers alight.

Some go to washroom, some buy food,
Some get settled in for good.
The bus people ensure everything is OK,
Productive use they make of the short stay.
Everything accounted for, let's make a move,
Pretty soon the bus is in its groove.
After a few hours, there's another break,
Mostly for the drivers to dinner take.
Others get down to go to the loo,
And do whatever it is they have to do.
Everything done, the bus moves again,
This time there's no stopping, my friend.
The driver and conductor, awake they stay,
While the passengers try to rest away.
The bunk is small, the space is cramped,
To read there is an overhead lamp.
To charge your phone there is a socket,
Just take your charger and simply plug it.
Bedding and pillow and linen provided,
So too is some sort of a blanket.
Any bumps in the road, the bus hits flat,
It is air-conditioned, so at least there's that.
Over the window, you can draw a curtain,
Light will still filter through, that is certain.
The bumps on the road make it hard to sleep,
The rumble of the engine does company keep.
Don't wear shoes while you're on the bunk,
Dirt, mud, slime, it'll bring all the gunk.
It's really tiring writing in this dim light,

Stop now I will, and I just might.
Get a few winks now, get some sleep,
And hope this tiredness makes it deep.

Scribbles… At a Petrol Pump

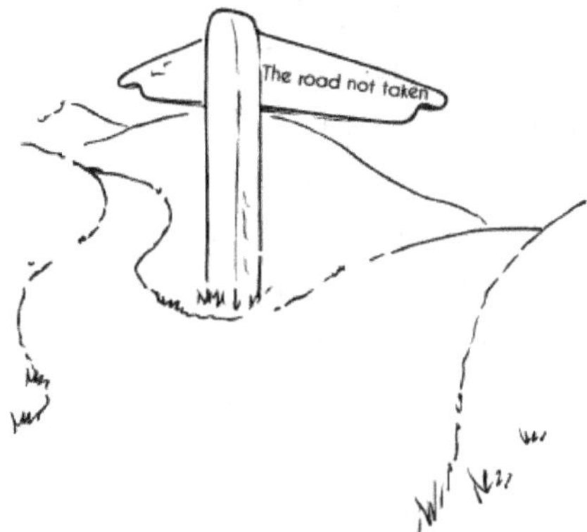

I'm at a petrol pump trying to fill up with fuel,
And this world in itself can be so cruel.
Just on the day that I'm in a hurry,
There's a huge crowd that's making me worry.
Whether I'll reach my destination on time,
Or be delayed through no fault of mine.
Whatever the case, I'm stuck here now,
I have to pass my time somehow.
One thing, however, that I'm knowing,
With a naked flame, you should not be going.
What could be the cause of such a crowd?
Fuel prices aren't even rising as of now.
Usually, if the prices will rise,
On the next day, then it would suffice.
That everyone wants to fill up before,
And not risk having to pay up more.

But nothing like that is happening tomorrow,
So why am I faced with misery and sorrow?
A young couple sitting on a bike,
May be going out for dinner tonight.
A family with kids in the backseat,
Turn on the AC to beat the heat.
The kids look bored just sitting there,
Maybe to have fun they'll go somewhere.
Another SUV with a group of eight,
Wherever they're going, they're gonna be late.
Some people talking on a mobile phone,
Even after suggesting it's not to be done.
A standard pump has fuel of two types,
And it goes on through the days and the nights.
Some pumps may also have CNG,
That one has its separate pump, usually.
Petrol and diesel are the two fuels,
If you mix them, you'd look like fools.
Fill the correct one inside your car,
Otherwise, it will not go very far.
Fuel is quite expensive these days,
You still have to fill it up anyways.
A group of friends may have just one,
Or two bikes amongst the lot of them.
The others make a contribution,
For gathering funds, that's their solution.
Old people having a serious discussion,
About the economy and its condition.

When you reach the nozzle, you check the meter,
Fuel is poured in by the litre.
More often than not, some of it gets spilt,
Then you're given some sort of a bill.
Use UPI or cash or card,
Some places have a loyalty card.
Pay it up, and you're on your way,
To drive around 'til the end of the day.
You can top up all your tires with air,
To correct pressure at the front and the rear.
You may also need to update your PUC,
To do that, the process is really easy.
Take your vehicle to the correct spot,
Put a probe down its exhaust.
Turn it on and wait a few seconds,
For the system to take measurements.
Take a photo of your number plate,
Get a printout with an expiry date.
Engine oil and lubricants are also sold,
Especially for the vehicles that are very old.
You may even have a grocery store,
To spend your time if you are bored.
Snacks, soft drinks, and ice creams too,
Things you can eat on-the-go.
Fuel is something we take for granted,
But good care, however, is warranted.
Fuel which is needed for any endeavour,
Once it's wasted, is lost forever.

Scribbles... In Traffic

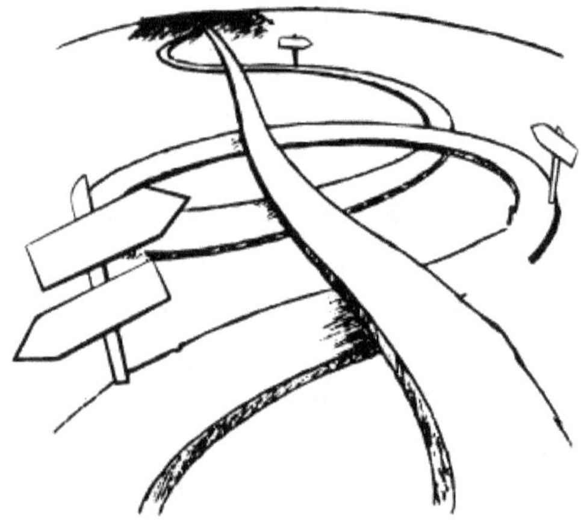

OK, so this may take a while,
This thing is nearly as long as the Nile.
Something big must have happened,
Everyone's spirits this has dampened.
I'm stuck in traffic, in case you're wondering,
There's a slight drizzle, there's no thundering.
Nature doesn't seem to have any part played,
The cause of this appears to be man-made.
I wonder how long we'll be stuck like this,
People are their appointments gonna miss.
Someone might be on their way,

To have a meeting later in the day.
Others to an airport might be going,
Hope they left on time, perfectly knowing,
That a distinct possibility exists,
Of there occurring something like this.
Someone might be on their way home,
Extremely tired, down to the bone.
At least there is no ambulance stuck,
So there is no one with such bad luck.
Kids in cars getting bored,
To keep them entertained, stories are being told.
There's also trucks and lorries and bus,
An assortment of vehicles there is thus.
Everyone is going to be late,
This thing will not soon abate.
Everyone moves, but no one gets anywhere,
That's what is meant by commute everywhere.
It'll take a miracle to get out of this,
I hope to God I don't need to piss.
There's nowhere for anyone to go,
The way this is moving, so slow.
It's not fully stationary, by God's grace,
It's moving forwards at a snail's pace.
Who, what, why, I begin to wonder,
Who has made such a big blunder?
Have two cars come together head-on,
Maybe because they didn't warn,
Of their presence at an unsighted bend,
And didn't have time for their actions to mend?

Maybe it's a lorry that has broken down,
With its driver clueless, carrying a frown.
A mechanic may then have to come,
And do what it is that needs to be done.
Or maybe some cargo's fallen over,
Unlashed, in a truck, without a cover.
Maybe someone has missed their mark,
And put it in a ditch, just for a lark.
We've now moved closer, so hopefully we'll see,
What's the exact cause of this, Gee!
Roadworks! Now? In this sort of place?
As it is, everyone's struggling for space.
In this place, if you really had to work,
You could've done it after dark.
At a time when the traffic is less,
It would have avoided this big mess.
Anyway, we're out now, let's go away,
Try and make up time along the way.
This traffic jam was a lot of stress,
Thankfully, it's over now. God Bless!

Scribbles... In a Bank

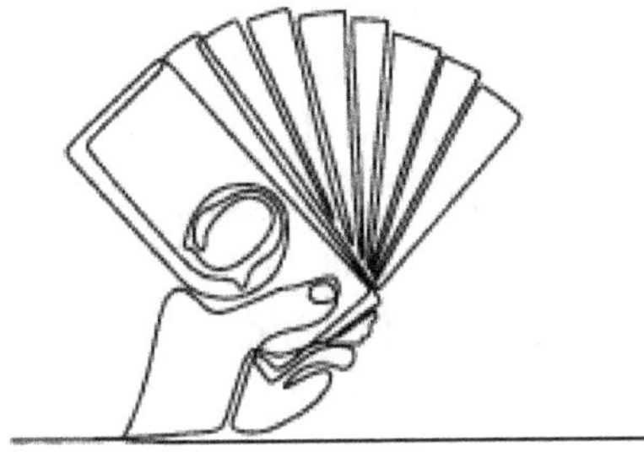

Oh, Dear! I don't know how to explain this,
But something, somewhere is amiss.
My account is stuck, and I don't know how,
It could even be possible somehow.
It was working up to two days ago,
All of a sudden it decided to go.
So, here I am, in a place called a bank,
To find out whom do I have to thank.
For this problem, a major inconvenience,
But to do this, you need good resilience.
For, you see, the process is slow,
And most of the time, they themselves don't
know.
Most of the time, the server is down,
People behind the counter always wearing a
frown.
Many people here, each with his own problem,
Trying to know how each one could solve them.

Somebody's cheque book hasn't yet arrived,
Someone's account balance has nosedived.
He seems convinced he didn't withdraw,
Any money from the said account at all.
Someone's debit card is stuck in the mail,
This is his third visit, his life is hell.
In spite of inputting the correct password,
Your net banking is blocked, which is weird.
Old people who don't even have a smartphone,
Can't install the app and transact from home.
The online system has become deranged,
Someone's registered mobile number just
changed.
He's been using the same for more than ten
years,
What if someone else accesses his account, he
fears.
Trying to make you invest in an FD,
To meet their targets is their strategy.
Some even have credit cards for you,
Earn and spend, and pay your dues.
Safe deposit vaults for your valuables,
Yet to fill out a form, there's hardly a table.
With billions of bucks, these people are dealing,
With a string, tie a pen to prevent you from
stealing.
Don't even think about taking out a loan,
Lest you end up losing everything you own.
Someone's trying to deposit some cash,

There's so much paper, so much trash.
In a separate machine, you update your passbook,
By post, you receive a new cheque book.
Every time you sign, it appears different,
It doesn't match, are you a delinquent?
To get your turn, you take a token,
And wait for it to be called by a person.
In the PPF, you can also deposit,
Other schemes may exist, you won't even know it.
Go from one counter to another,
Just to get all your documents in order.
You still need to do your KYC,
So it can be confirmed, you are who they see.
The manager sits in a separate cabin,
A big discussion he seems to be having.
A separate vestibule has an ATM,
To take out cash with a dedicated PIN.
It is out of order quite a lot of times,
You've just gone and wasted your time.
A security guard without a gun,
In case of a robbery, just run.
And although this thing might sound a little funny,
A bank still might be your safest bet to handle your money.

Scribbles... In an Exam Hall

Okay, so here I am, sitting in the hall,
Awaiting my turn, waiting for a call.
It's my viva, or oral exam if you will,
But right now I have some time to kill.
For, you see, the examiner is late,
But us, examinees, have to follow the time and
date.
If they are late, it's OK, it's all fine,
But if the roles are reversed, you may fail this
time.
They can be late, they're human, what to do?
God forbid that you're late, how dare you?
Now, you may wonder why I'm writing this,
Especially when I have an exam in a few
minutes.

I should be studying, maybe reading some notes,
Or maybe think of a good anecdote.
But, you know, however the case may be,
Cramming last minute just isn't for me.
To each his own, that might be the case,
I just don't believe in being part of the race.
If what I have done so far isn't enough,
Well, then passing this is gonna be tough.
It's best to be calm and cool and collected,
And to let your mind do, of it what is expected.
I need to be calm just before the storm,
To not stress out, I make that a norm.
Plus, this provides a good distraction,
Rather than stress out and have a reaction.
There are other people here, having a seat,
All dressed up, proper, formal and neat.
Some are reading, trying to memorize,
Some look lost from the look in their eyes.
Some trying to practice what they want to be saying,
Some clearly look as if they're praying.
Tension seems to be the name of the game,
After today, their lives won't be the same.
One door opens, an examinee stumbles out,
This can't be happening, in his mind he seems to shout.
I've given it my all, I've struggled a lot,
There isn't anything that I could've forgot.
He seems to have failed, that's what it looks like,

The next guy goes in, balling his fists tight.
Others surround him, asking for some tips,
He gives them some with his hands on his hips.
It's a game of luck, a gamble, so to speak,
To be asked a question that you seek.
You may have studied the entire field,
But may be asked something completely
left-field.
Elsewhere you might have studied just a few,
And get asked exactly that which you knew.
It's like a lottery, some lose, some win,
The most important thing is to take it on the
chin.
Pick yourself up and try and try again,
This isn't the end of the world, my friend.
One exam may not determine your value,
It doesn't mean you take it lightly, mind you.
They've called my name, I'm going in next,
I suppose I should stop writing this text.
Why is my mouth suddenly devoid of saliva?
Don't you panic, man, this is just a viva.
Wish me luck, I really hope I pass it,
Well, you know what?

..

.

.

.

I Did!!

Scribbles... At a Conference

Boy, I'm tired, I have to sit down,
Take a breath, relax, look around.
Here I am at a technical conference,
Trying to learn, understand, make an inference.
This is not simply a roundtable discussion,
It also includes rounds of presentations.
People have written, based on research and
study,
A paper to present to the professional
community.
The topic of the paper has to be new,
It must go through various stages of review.
But the papers are not the main reason,
People are here for the exhibition.
It's the most important to tell you the truth,
Companies globally acquire a booth.

Depending on the size that you need,
More money you need to part with, please.
All in the hope to find a new client,
One, ten, hundred to make you a giant.
Put in the effort, show your work,
Marketing's key to show your worth.
Some have products, some services,
Some protect you from near-misses.
Visitors visiting each and every stall,
Profits can possibly rise or fall.
Meetings, chats, agreements and discussions,
To get maximum business is the mission.
For a whole day, you may have to stand,
Deals may be done through the shake of a hand.
Some have equipment for live demonstrations,
Some have samples to capture your attention.
Hand over business cards, pick up a brochure,
Promise to meet up in the near future.
Talks punctuated by coffee breaks,
A refreshing pause everybody takes.
Lunch is served, better stand in a queue,
Local delicacies with salad and stew.
Everyone starts queuing up early,
Already metres long, in five minutes barely.
With as much as you want, fill up a plate,
Food may run out, so don't be late.
Plate in hand, go find a table,
Stand and eat if you aren't able.
Paper presentations in a parallel session,

Four, maybe five, maybe six in succession.
Then there is the Gala Dinner,
The one session that is always a winner.
Usually held in the middle of the week,
With beer, wine, and drink non-alcoholic.
Select an option – vegan or meat,
Set menu available as printed on a sheet.
Senior officials invited on stage,
For brief introductions, short and not vague.
Live entertainment – dance and song,
If you feel like, do sing along.
There may even be a Cultural Night,
Local traditions just see you might.
Local games and art and dress,
To learn a new culture, this is the best.
Even at the start of the last day,
Everyone's packing, don't bother to stay.
The whole purpose of this exercise,
Was to grow your business, client-wise.
If it doesn't happen, don't dismiss this in haste,
The connections made here seldom go to waste.

Scribbles... Before a Meeting

I'm sitting in the lobby, waiting for a meeting,
And thinking about how many people I'll be
greeting.
The timing itself couldn't have been a better ask,
Just getting up here was a monumental task.
Heat, sweat, humidity at an all-time high,
Not to mention rain pouring from the sky.
External factors like these, yes, they were rough,
Just arranging the meeting itself was tough.
I had to go through hoops, just to get here,
While trying not to have even an ounce of fear.
Well, it worked, so here I am,
My point home now I have to ram.
Ten times I have gone through the presentation,
Tried to think about each and every question.
Whatever it is that they may try to ask,

Any subtle hints their queries may mask.
I hope I can answer every query properly,
Most, if not all, doubts solved clearly.
The meeting's been delayed by a fair few
minutes,
That's pretty much the norm these days, isn't it?
In another meeting, everyone is busy,
These thoughts in my head could make me
dizzy.
There's only so much I can think about this
meeting,
Any more than this and I'll start sweating.
That's why I'm writing this, as a distraction,
To keep myself calm, this is a course of action.
At least the waiting room is air-conditioned,
It certainly is helping me in my mission.
A couple of framed pictures of old architecture,
Another few paintings with a different texture.
Artificial plants kept in various places,
Chairs and tables occupy other spaces.
Certificates and achievements hung up on the
walls,
Pale pink wallpaper adorning the halls.
Magazines and newspapers on a coffee table,
A TV hanging opposite with a dangling cable.
The receptionist is busy, texting on her phone,
A few other people, chatting in a drone.
I was offered water when I sat down,
Followed by coffee, more white than brown.

I'm still focused on the job ahead,
In spite of the commotion going on in my head.
The intercom was buzzing, left, right and centre,
The receptionist had to put her phone down and
answer.
The other guys in the room have been called
inside,
As I continue to wait, my time I must bide.
Once again I go through my presentation,
Along with which I have a demonstration.
Mentally I check off all the points one by one,
Before coming, all the equipment I had run.
My phone is on silent so there's no disturbance,
I have tried to take each and every precaution.
If this isn't successful, it'll be a pity,
But if it is, it's a new opportunity.
I will go inside, and this meeting will be perfect,
And all the effort, stress and sweat will
definitely be worth it.

Scribbles... At a Racetrack

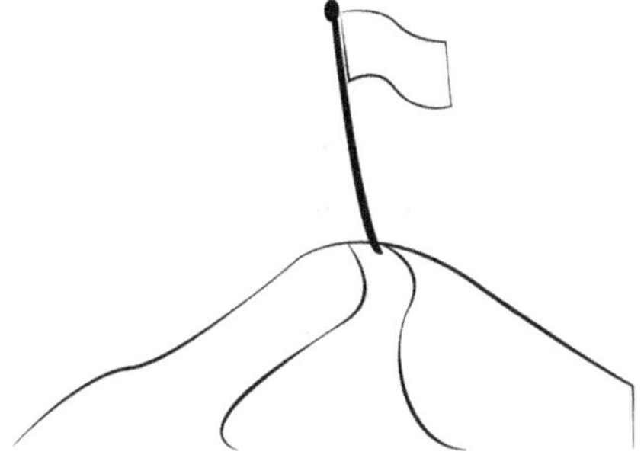

Wow! OK! I have to sit down now,
This was absolutely exhilarating, and how!
My heart is pumping, it is beating fast,
And I don't know how long it will last.
I don't remember ever having had such a thrill,
In what I did in the past or in the future will.
Being a VIP at a motor race,
Is a rare opportunity, by God's grace.
You get special access that takes you in,
The middle of the action, thick or thin.
Going behind the scenes, in the pit lane,
Is enough to make one go insane.
Seeing a racecar, up close and personal,
And perhaps touch it if it isn't illegal.
The mechanics work away, on the car tinkering,
Everything is OK, they are ensuring.
Brakes, steering, chassis, and temperature of
fuel,

And the pressure inside all four tyres too.
Then all of a sudden, she comes alive,
The roar of a V8 in front of your eyes.
Everything checked, the car up and ready,
Tools lying around, so you have to walk steady.
Go inside the hauler, where the crew sits,
It is also where they keep the car's spare bits.
You get a tour of the entire place,
Including that of the driver's personal space.
Fireproof overalls and helmets kept here,
And everything else that the driver holds dear.
In the briefing room, you sit on the couch,
As you are explained all the ins-and-outs.
You are even provided with some free drinks,
And goodie bags full of fancy things.
T-shirts, caps, and other official merch,
Things you won't find no matter how much you
search.
You walk out to the middle of the track,
Leaving your luggage right at the back.
You meet your team's drivers, who will drive the
car,
Chat with them, wish them luck, hope they go
far.
Of course, this is when you get their autograph,
On your tee, pass, paper, or even on your cap.
Also, remember to take pictures too,
With the driver, car and the pit crew.
You meet other drivers at their introduction,

And stand still for the national anthem.
If you're lucky, you may get a car-to-pit radio,
And listen to every conversation on the go.
You make your way onto the team's pit wall,
The best vantage point to feel it all.
Make sure you have your earmuffs,
Thirty Eight V8s can sound pretty rough.
The lights go green, the race is a go,
In front of your eyes, everything unfolds.
Two hundred miles an hour on the same piece of
track,
The drivers thread their way through a reducing
gap.
These machines are some of the best,
In case of an accident, they are the safest.
You hold your breath as your guy pits,
Change tyres and refuel in under a minute.
As the drivers leave their pit mark,
The smell of burning rubber goes straight to
your heart.
Through all this, you are always listening,
What the pit crew and the driver are saying.
Two hundred laps and the race is done,
A hundred twenty minutes of adrenaline and
fun.
Now I'm sitting down at the back of the hauler,
As they bring the cars back to the trailer.
Being a main sponsor of a racing car,
It just makes you feel like a star.

For a lifelong fan of racing, just like me,
This is something great, as great as great can be.
Not only is it unique, not only is it new,
For someone like me, it's a childhood dream
come true.

Scribbles... At an Amusement Park

An amusement park is a place to see,
Kids and adults and even teens.
It's a place that's open for everyone,
To come and enjoy and have fun.
For kids, it's a chance to find some joy,
For teens to behave like a boy.
For adults, it's a chance to forget everything,
And connect with the child lying dormant
within.
A one-time paid ticket allows you to,
Go on every ride that you want to.
However, you may have to stand in a queue,
And there are height restrictions for small kids
too.

Some rides are easy, like the carousel,
Anyone can get on just as well.
Others such as the Ferris wheel,
Also aren't worth much of a deal.
Roller coasters may not be everyone's cup of
tea,
There are different types, some hard, some scary.
On some rides, you can take the whole family,
On others all alone in a seat, you have to be.
Handlebars and seat belts keep you safe,
Loose items to be kept in a separate safe.
Even if the coaster doesn't make you scared,
On it you should shout, it is recommended.
It just adds to the feel of things,
It doesn't matter what you're shouting.
Some amusement parks may even have a
mascot,
Whose job includes making people laugh a lot.
You have to feel for the person inside the suit,
It's hot and stuffy and perhaps sweaty too.
There are lots of places for you to get some
food,
Some really elegant, some not so good.
Restaurants, eateries, cafes, or just a stand,
You can eat with knife and fork, or maybe just
your hand.
From around the world different types of
cuisine,
You decide what it is you want to put in.

Pizza, burger, salad, or some other fast food,
Or maybe some wine to get yourself in the
mood.
Exquisite restaurants that cater to your taste,
Japanese sushi with Wasabi paste.
You even have a lot of options for dessert,
To let the kid inside you go absolutely berserk.
The park is open in almost every season,
To ensure that you do not need a reason.
In the summer heat, you can have yourself a
beer,
Maybe in the winter, you can spread the
Christmas cheer.
But the food in itself is not free,
You will have to part with more of your money.
In the blazing heat, you may have to stand,
To see the live performance of the in-house
band.
It's not just the food, there's more to it than that,
You could lose more money at the drop of a hat.
I'm of course talking about the different types of
shops,
Luring you in and enticing you to
shop-till-you-drop.
At the exit of every ride you go,
You will find its dedicated merchandise store.
There also are some other shops lying around,
Selling stuff to which no relation is found.

A souvenir is something every child wants to
have,
To celebrate and remember the day that they've
just had.
The park is a place to meet with family,
Some distant cousins or a nephew and a niece.
Grandparents and grandkids enjoying together,
Or young couples simply enjoying the weather.
Some people may even bring along a pet,
School and studies all the children forget.
Even the ones who are differently abled,
Of having a good time they are capable.
It's funny how a place that is meant to amuse,
Can also sometimes leave you bemused.
Even the coldest, meanest person manages to
find,
Something in this place to pacify their innermost
child.

Scribbles… In a Shopping Mall

The place that is known as a shopping mall,
Is a place where you can get anything at all.
A majority of shops selling lots of clothes,
From two to ninety can get their robes.
Shirts, tees, trousers, or jeans instead,
For men the options are limited.
With the occasional coat, belt and tie,
That's all there is to a man's attire.
For women, there are options aplenty,
Different types, at least twenty.
And don't you forget the little kids,
They too have their very own fits.
Not just that, they have their own store,
With shoes and socks and clothes shand more.

It makes me wonder about the cloth,
Where does it come from, how is it got?
And what is the process that it goes through,
Before being available for you to use?
And the dye that is used to give a colour,
In different shades for different fervour.
You can try your clothes in a changing room,
To ensure you buy a size that fits you.
Then there's footwear of rubber and leather,
Built to withstand any sort of weather.
Malls also sell various accessories,
From souvenirs to precious jewellery.
Souvenirs like local handicrafts,
From the local town that the mall is a part.
Platinum, silver, diamond and gold,
Jewellery in various forms is sold.
Watchmakers trying to sell you time,
A thing more valuable than its price in dimes.
There are also places where you get food,
After walking a lot, to make you feel good.
Eateries, restaurants and a café,
Selling different foods, night and day.
Eat what you feel, what your heart craves,
Burgers and fries and pizza and shakes.
Maybe some Indian or some Chinese,
Maybe Korean or some Lebanese.
There are also quite a few movie screens,
For you to enjoy some colourful scenes.
Snacks, popcorn and soda pop,

Take your seats before the lights drop.
Special shops selling ice cream and candy,
Little kids feeling happy and dandy.
There may even be a shop selling toys,
For babies, toddlers, girls and boys.
Full-grown adults can also feel good,
And get a chance to relive their childhood.
There even is a big bookstore,
Fiction, non-fiction and tales of lore.
Books for the young and the old alike,
Grab what you want, read what you like.
There also may be a gaming zone,
To enjoy with friends or on your own.
Spend your time at the bowling alley,
Arcade, e-sports, or just dilly-dally.
Vehicle parking on multiple levels,
To find one empty move around in circles.
Going to a mall is a different experience,
Where people go to be unserious.
A place that used to be used for leisure,
Has now formed its very own culture.

Scribbles... In a Restaurant

Came out to eat today, just for a lark,
As usual, I couldn't find a place to park.
Found a spot a fair bit of distance afar,
Then had to wait for nearly an hour.
So many people coming out to eat,
How is everyone gonna get a seat?
Didn't feel like going to another place,
For I was craving something from this place.
And even if I had decided to change,
It wouldn't have at all been so strange.
If I'd had to wait even longer than now,

Even if I'd found a table somehow.
People go out for various reasons,
It doesn't matter what time or season.
Some go alone to get some me time,
Some celebrate earning their first dime.
Birthdays are a time to go out,
Anniversaries too, without a doubt.
Long-lost friends catching up,
Heated discussions ramping up.
People going out on a romantic date,
Some do so because they're late.
Perhaps they're out because they're bored.
Or maybe good grades they have scored.
Got your first job, that's so great,
Only one thing to do – celebrate.
A group of friends, looking to hang out,
Talking so loud, appearing to shout.
Business deals made over wine,
Take your clients out to dine.
Different foods, different people order,
Mix and match, without a border.
Everyone knows what they like best,
It may not match with that of their guest.
Multi-cuisine is what is found,
In most restaurants up and down.
People usually start with a drink,
Just so it gives them some time to think.
Someone takes an extra ice cube,
Someone else fancies some hot soup.

Peanuts, cheese, or maybe some sev,
Complimentary snacks they usually give.
Appetizers also they can bring,
Whatever you want, just order the thing.
Some people stop with just the hors d'oeuvres,
Others move on to the main course.
This is where the most variety is seen,
Roti-subzi-rice to chow-mein.
Risotto, pasta, penne, ravioli,
Gnocchi, arrabbiata, or aioli,
Sushi, tortilla, or some tacos,
With guacamole as dip to a side of nachos.
Vegetable and meat, both are available,
Piping hot they are brought to your table.
After the entrée, it's time for dessert,
Pudding, cake, or a flavoured yoghurt.
Or maybe you can have a scoop of ice-cream,
Simple yet effective, tastes like a dream.
Please don't let anything go to waste,
It shows your upbringing, shows your taste.
Eat what you want, order only what you can
Finish; and not throw anything away, man.
Because you know, this is the deal,
Some people can't afford even one day's meal.

Scribbles... At the Vet

I've come with my boy to the vet,
But our number hasn't come yet.
Notice how I called him boy, and not dog,
He's worth more than anything I've got.
Both don't like coming here, him and I,
Both have our different reasons why.
He doesn't like the needle's prick,
Although it ensures he doesn't fall sick.
I don't like seeing animals in pain,
Some very thin, some with weight gain.
Not that he likes that, he doesn't too,
He understands this much more than I do.
My boy's friendly, he wants to meet,
Every animal that comes he wants to greet.

I try to keep him safe, keep him away,
Others may be having a pretty rough day.
A small, young puppy visiting for the first time,
To get vaccinated, to be healthy and fine.
Someone's got a cat in a backpack,
Hoisting it on their very own back.
Some dog's got a broken leg,
With paw in a cast, he can't walk straight.
Another one's got a tick infection,
For that, he's here to take an injection.
There's even a turtle in a small box,
Its shell pretty hard, hard as a rock.
A few other scenes that are hard to describe,
So sad that they might just kill the vibe.
A good, old girl, struggling to walk,
To climb a flight of stairs, she had to stop.
Another boy bleeding from his nose,
Whatever's gone wrong, I hope the vet knows.
At least no one's here to put their pet down,
That would've wrecked me, I'd have broken
down.
Just for the sake of it, don't get a pet,
Don't ever subject it to any neglect.
Don't get a dog just on a whim,
If proper care you can't take of him.
It's not a toy, it's a living being,
Who gives you more than you can ever give
him.
Love, care, compassion and empathy,

And whenever you need it, you'll also get sympathy.
Pets understand more than you ever could,
Treat them with respect, as everyone should.
Even the ones who live on the street,
Have a divine right to live with dignity.
Take some time out to try and understand,
To figure out where these beings stand.
They're smarter than most humans could ever be,
Take your time to know them, then you'll see.
Even if you can't be bothered to know them,
The least you can do is not go hurt them.
Theirs is a pure and innocent soul,
And their heart is made up of pure gold.
They're better living beings than humans can ever be,
You can't buy what they have with intelligence and money.
I hug my boy, and I hold him tight,
And promise to love him till the end of the light.
Every time I see an animal in trouble,
I promise to love my boy more than double.
As we go inside, our number is next,
I wish every animal all the very best.
You're all too precious to be living in this world,
Humans don't deserve such a good boy or girl.

Scribbles... In a Hospital

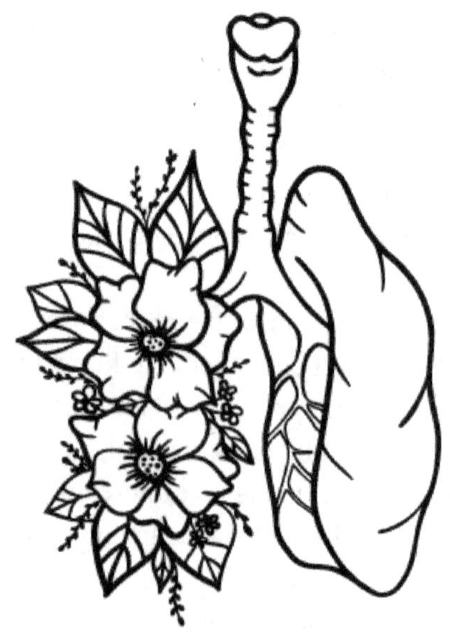

I'm sitting outside, they've been taken in,
And my patience now is wearing thin.
After all, you know, there's nothing to worry,
You still wish that the doctors would hurry.
Now that we know they're out of danger,
I can focus on looking at another stranger.
This place is scary, and it can be overwhelming,
Especially the more deeper that you start
delving.
In the same building where a mother gives birth,
Someone visits a doctor 'coz their tonsils hurt.

A broken bone can be seen in an X-ray,
And OPD lets you go in less than one day.
The despair of knowing there may be more to
come,
To the joy of knowing you're about to go home.
In the same place where a baby takes its first
breath,
Some people come to terms with a loved one's
death.
In the recovery from a massive accident,
Someone's using insurance to pay the room rent.
Illness and disease know no friend,
The poor and the rich, it affects all men.
The stress in the eyes of a next of kin,
Who's just been told that the chance is thin.
The jubilation in knowing everything's alright,
You're gonna last the day, fight another fight.
Somebody is having an ear to listen to,
A privilege found by a select few.
This place in itself is so depressing,
Enough to make sad the world's happiest being.
Being in good physical and mental health,
Is truly a sign of enormous wealth.
We only appreciate a part, when it's in pain,
Albeit temporary, a new perspective we gain.
No one in their right state of mind would ever
wish,
To visit this place, nor would they ever miss.
They've been discharged, it's such a relief,

My thoughts and prayers go to those in grief.
In no place of worship will you ever see,
And definitely not anywhere else you'll be.
Only in a hospital's thick, dense air,
Will you ever find the most heartfelt prayer.

Scribbles... During Covid Vaccination

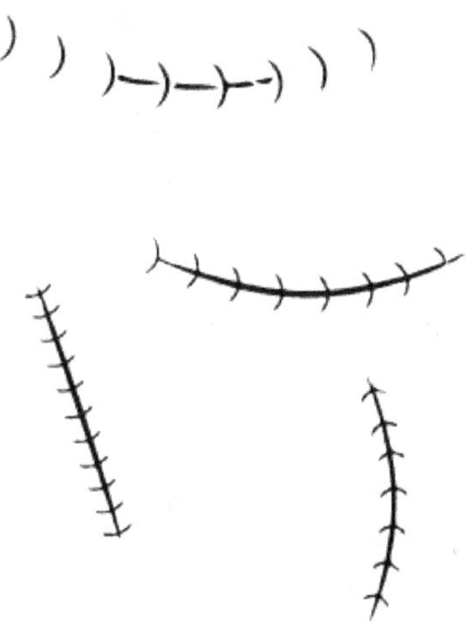

Nobody would've thought in their wildest
dreams,
That they'd ever be a part of such a scene.
Who would've imagined a few years back,
There would happen something that,
Would cause the world to come to a standstill,
From China to Europe all the way to Brazil.
What people thought was a simple virus,
Will sweep through and affect all of us.
Most of the world hadn't heard of a pandemic,

And now they were all stuck in the middle of it.
People fell ill and were hospitalized,
And before you knew it, many had died.
Hospitals were full, including ICU,
People isolated in their own homes too.
Social distancing was the phrase of the day,
A phrase that was used every single day.
Schools, colleges and offices shut,
With trains, flights, taxis and bus.
People were forced into lockdown,
People's worlds turned upside down.
Everyone forced to stay at home,
Unless something essential had to be done.
You could go to a clinic, you could go to a vet,
To buy medicines – for yourself or your pet.
Groceries open for a limited time,
Everyone outside had to stand in a line.
Pet supplies were open too,
For everything else you had to,
Wait for it to open, or order online,
Only delivery, don't stay and dine.
One wave came and one wave went,
The virus, however, wouldn't relent.
Wave after wave just came and hit,
Delta, Omicron, and other variant.
Some people did break the rules,
And showed the world that they were fools.
People hoped that this would end,
And they could try their lives to mend.

Companies developed the vaccination,
Governments urged citizens to take them.
Availability of more than one make,
You had to decide which one to take.
Not all countries accepted both,
Both seemed equally effective, though.
You had to book a slot online,
Search continuously all the time.
If you did manage to find a slot,
Consider yourself lucky that you even got.
Some people searched for days on end,
Others found it in a fraction of a second.
Take a printout of your confirmation,
At the scheduled time, go for vaccination.
Fill out some forms, wait in line,
They'd call you in, ten at a time.
Every shot had some side effects,
Fever, loose motions, overall weakness.
Bear with them, and you'll be fine,
Continue following precautions all the time.
After a few months, take shot number two,
This time though, things were better for you.
The waves had subsided, things were better,
You still had to take care of each other.
Continue to wear a mask covering nose and
mouth,
And sanitize your hands without a doubt.
One year later you take a booster shot,
This time though, things aren't so hot.

That is where I am, awaiting my turn.
And blessed that no one I know is in an urn.
Condolences to those who lost a loved one,
Just remember that your life isn't done.
Just breathe easy and let out a roar,
And tell the whole world, you're a survivor!

Scribbles... In a Temple

Woke up pretty early, then I had a bath,
Then I drove along the beaten path.
Got down a fair bit of distance away,
Then on foot, we made our way.
Outside the gate, you remove your footwear,
Wearing it inside is not allowed anywhere.
Along with it also, you have to deposit,
Your mobile phones and other electronics.
You are allowed, however, to carry your wallet,
And all the stuff that you carry in it.
In some places, you pass security,
In some others, there isn't any.
You walk along a pathway, some covered, some
bare,
And reach the main gate with a flight of stairs.
You are not alone, there is a huge crowd,
Quite a few people chanting out loud.
If everyone walks smoothly, you move fast,
Like a river flowing through the Western Ghats.

In the middle, however, if people stop,
Everything behind then gets bottled up.
And if someone in the middle decides to kneel,
And then starts praying with utmost zeal,
Then the crowd, which is already substantial,
May just come to a complete standstill.
Based on what time you reach the temple,
You may just be able to get a sample.
Of the morning prayer, or 'pooja' if you will,
Although you may have to stand outside the
grille.
You can hear the conch, you can hear the gong,
You can hear the trumpet and the vocal song.
The priests inside would have lit a fire,
And are throwing holy bits in the holy pyre.
They may also be, with water, the Lord bathing,
And then in his favourite clothes, they will dress
him.
Mostly this is done behind closed doors,
As the people outside start to get bored.
Some sing along if they know the hymn,
Others just clap along with the rhythm.
Some simply chant the holy God's name,
Who can shout the loudest, they all play a game.
Once the prayer's done, the big doors will open,
People rush inside so the Lord can greet them.
Be careful now, you might just get hurt,
In a rush to see who gets in there first.
Police and security, guarding everything,

No one is allowed to get close to Him,
Some people have brought plates of offerings,
The priests inside the temple those are gathering.
They keep most of it and then return some,
As if God is blessing the giving one.
Some people just give a bunch of cash,
Others anoint themselves with a bit of ash.
Just for a few seconds, you get to see,
His graceful face in all its glory.
You're quickly moved away, so the ones behind,
Can get their chance to worship the divine.
Some people come out, and for a while they sit,
Others make their way straight to the exit.
As you make your way back to where you kept
everything,
You just cannot help it and you start wondering.
So many people from various backgrounds,
Yet all are equal inside this holy ground.
Because one thing, in the end, is true,
Faith has no boundaries like religions do.

Scribbles… During Voting

Every few years a time does come,
When one has to weigh the pros and cons.
Of what has happened in the past few years,
And where do they want to go from here.
In any place where there is a Democracy,
Citizens play an important role, you see.
To control the future, they have the power,
To decide how a country should flower.
Citizens have an important obligation,
To cast their vote and steer their nation.
Your voting centre may be in a different city,
From your office or your university.
The dates for voting are announced in advance,
So that you have enough time to make plans.
Take time out and visit the centre,
And go to the room you're supposed to enter.
If you're lucky, there won't be a queue,
Although, most likely, there will be too.

Await your turn, stand in a queue,
There really isn't anything much you can do.
Other people like you, standing in line,
From their busy schedule, taking out the time.
Some young ones casting their vote,
For the very first time, giving it some thought.
They may be between eighteen and twenty-two,
They are, however, doing their bit too.
At the other end are the seniors,
Who have been doing this for years.
Some come alone, some together,
Some come braving inclement weather.
Some people arriving in a wheelchair,
Just to do their duty, they have dared.
To the front of the queue, they are sent,
So that they don't have to wait till day's end.
Youngsters bored, playing on their phones,
Seasoned ones talking in a monotone.
Discussing their views, sharing opinions,
The what, the who, the where and the when.
In every center, there's more than one room,
Go to the correct one, do not assume.
As luck would have it, my queue is long,
And it doesn't seem to be moving along.
The room next door is nearly empty,
A small number of people, less than twenty.
A big piece of paper stuck on the wall,
With names and symbols like a roll call.
In big letters is printed – Sample,

Lest you see it and take a gamble.
Soon I'll go in, and they'll verify,
With an ID that it is indeed I.
Make me write my name in a register,
And then send me to the next counter.
To confirm that I have cast my vote,
They will in their list make a note.
With indelible ink they'll mark my finger,
The ink won't go until November.
Then they'll take me to the polling booth,
And show me how to press the button I choose.
I'll wait for them to move away,
And then press the button that I may,
Feel like pressing, and then I'm done,
I'll make way for the next one.
Do their duty, everyone must,
Try to be fair, try to be just.
People who don't give their say,
Can't really complain at the end of the day.
'Coz for the betterment of their own country,
Casting their vote is every citizen's duty.